THIS BOOK BELONGS TO:

_____

THE WONDERFUL WORLD OF FROGS

Mimi Jones

Dedicated to all the frog lovers.

ISBN 978-1-958985-41-0

www.joeysavestheday.com

A Mimi Book

WELCOME TO THE WONDERFUL WORLD OF FROGS

Frogs are amphibians, meaning they can live in water and on land.

Frogs have smooth, moist skin that helps them breathe through their skin.

breathe

Tadpoles

Frogs lay their eggs in water, and these eggs hatch into tadpoles.

Tadpoles have tails and gills, allowing them to swim and breathe underwater.

As tadpoles grow, they undergo metamorphosis, developing legs and losing their tails to become adult frogs.

Frogs have long, sticky tongues that they use to catch insects and other prey.

Some frog species can jump up to 20 times their body length in a single leap!

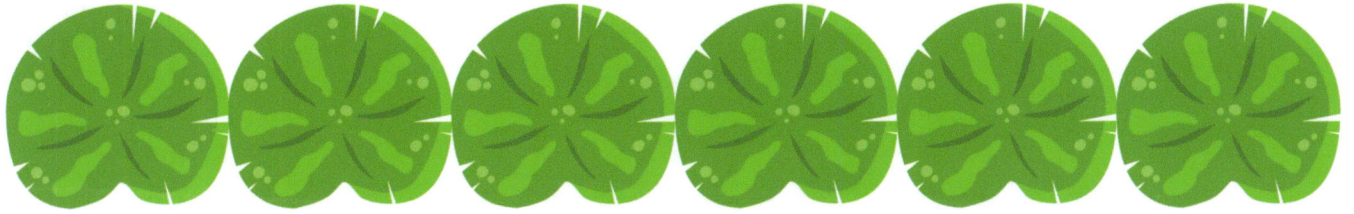

Frogs come in various colors, from bright greens and yellows to deep reds and blues.

The bright colors of some frogs, like the poison dart frog, serve as a warning to predators that they are toxic.

Frogs have excellent night vision, which helps them hunt in low light conditions.

Vision

Frogs are found on every continent except Antarctica.

Frogs can absorb water through their skin, so they don't need to drink through their mouths.

The Paedophryne amauensis holds the title for the world's tiniest frog, measuring in at under half an inch in length.

Also known as the New Guinea Amau frog.

The largest frog is the Goliath frog, which can grow up to 12.5 inches in length.

LARGEST

Some frogs can change color to blend in with their surroundings, a process called camouflage.

CROAK

CHiRP

Frogs communicate using a variety of vocalizations, including croaks, chirps, and trills.

Some species of frogs, like the glass frog, have translucent skin that allows you to see their internal organs.

Frogs have powerful hind legs that are well-adapted for jumping and swimming.

Frogs' eyes are positioned on the top of their heads, giving them a wide field of vision.

Vision

Some frogs have developed unique ways to carry their eggs, like the Surinam toad, which carries eggs on its back.

The golden poison dart frog ranks among the most toxic creatures on the planet, possessing enough venom to potentially kill ten humans.

Frogs play a vital role in their ecosystems by controlling insect populations and serving as prey for other animals.

SENSITIVE

Frogs are sensitive to environmental changes and are often used as indicators of ecosystem health.

Freeze

Some frogs can survive freezing temperatures by producing a type of natural antifreeze in their bodies.

Frogs use their eyes to help swallow food by pushing their eyes down into their mouths.

Frogs have a unique way of breathing called buccal pumping, where they use their throat muscles to move air in and out of their lungs.

breathe

Count the frogs.

Thank you for taking the time to read this. I hope you found it informative and gained some valuable insights.

The End!